PRINCEWILL LAGANG

Solving Tomorrow's Problems: Innovation for Entrepreneurs

First published by PRINCEWILL LAGANG 2023

Copyright © 2023 by Princewill Lagang

All rights reserved. No part of this publication may be reproduced, stored or transmitted in any form or by any means, electronic, mechanical, photocopying, recording, scanning, or otherwise without written permission from the publisher. It is illegal to copy this book, post it to a website, or distribute it by any other means without permission.

Princewill Lagang asserts the moral right to be identified as the author of this work.

First edition

This book was professionally typeset on Reedsy.
Find out more at reedsy.com

Contents

1. Solving Tomorrow's Problems: Innovation for Entrepreneurs ... 1
2. Navigating the Innovation Landscape ... 5
3. Ideation and Creativity: Seeds of Innovation ... 9
4. From Idea to Execution: Building Your Innovation ... 12
5. Market Entry and Innovation Adoption ... 16
6. Innovation and Sustainability: Making a Lasting Impact ... 19
7. Innovation in a Changing World: Adapting to Challenges ... 23
8. Innovation for the Future: Trends and Emerging Opportunities ... 26
9. Innovation for Impact: Making a Difference in the World ... 30
10. The Entrepreneur's Toolkit: Strategies for Success ... 33
11. Beyond Entrepreneurship: Scaling and Legacy ... 37
12. Summary ... 40

1

Solving Tomorrow's Problems: Innovation for Entrepreneurs

The sun was just beginning to cast long shadows across the bustling cityscape as Mark Harrison, a young entrepreneur with a vision, sat down at his favorite coffee shop. With his laptop open and a steaming cappuccino in hand, he couldn't help but feel a surge of excitement as he contemplated the journey that lay ahead. This was the start of a new chapter, one filled with challenges, opportunities, and the promise of making a meaningful impact on the world.

The coffee shop was abuzz with the energy of the morning rush. Baristas expertly crafted espresso drinks, while patrons hunched over laptops and scribbled notes in leather-bound journals. Mark took a sip of his cappuccino and gazed out of the window at the towering skyscrapers that surrounded him. It was a reminder of the ever-changing landscape of the business world, and the need for innovation to thrive in this environment.

Innovation was a term often thrown around in the world of entrepreneurship, but what did it truly mean? How could Mark and other aspiring entrepreneurs harness the power of innovation to tackle the challenges of tomorrow and create successful businesses? These questions had been swirling in Mark's mind for quite some time, and he was determined to find answers.

As he opened his laptop, Mark began to type a list of questions and ideas, eager to explore the concept of innovation and its role in the entrepreneurial journey. He knew that understanding innovation was the key to building a business that not only survived but thrived in an ever-evolving marketplace. This chapter, "Solving Tomorrow's Problems: Innovation for Entrepreneurs," would serve as a roadmap for Mark and anyone who sought to embark on the entrepreneurial adventure.

The Essence of Innovation

Innovation was not just about creating groundbreaking technology or launching a disruptive product; it was a mindset, a way of thinking and problem-solving that could be applied to any aspect of business. Mark believed that, at its core, innovation was about finding creative solutions to the challenges and opportunities presented by an ever-changing world.

In the past, innovation was often associated with large corporations and well-funded research and development departments. However, Mark knew that innovation was not the exclusive domain of these giants. Entrepreneurs, with their agility, determination, and passion, had a unique advantage in the world of innovation. They could pivot quickly, take calculated risks, and turn ideas into reality with limited resources.

As Mark delved into his research, he discovered that innovation was not a one-size-fits-all concept. It could take many forms, from incremental improvements to radical breakthroughs. It encompassed product innovation, process innovation, business model innovation, and even social innovation. Mark was determined to explore each facet and understand how they could be harnessed for entrepreneurial success.

The Evolution of Entrepreneurship

The world had seen a significant shift in the way entrepreneurs operated in recent years. The traditional model of building a business around a single static idea was becoming increasingly outdated. Today's entrepreneurs needed to be adaptable, constantly learning, and prepared to pivot when necessary. Mark believed that this new breed of entrepreneur was an innovator by nature, always seeking new ways to solve problems and capture opportunities.

Mark had seen countless examples of entrepreneurs who started with one idea, only to pivot and find success in a completely different direction. This adaptability was a testament to the power of innovation and the ability to remain agile in the face of uncertainty. To Mark, the ability to solve tomorrow's problems lay in an entrepreneur's capacity to innovate, evolve, and learn from both successes and failures.

The Entrepreneur's Toolkit

In his research, Mark discovered that there were specific tools and strategies that could help entrepreneurs become more innovative. These included design thinking, problem-solving frameworks, ideation techniques, and the power of collaboration. Mark knew that these tools were not reserved for a select few; they could be learned and applied by anyone willing to invest the time and effort.

Mark believed that this chapter would serve as a guide, offering practical insights and real-world examples to help aspiring entrepreneurs embrace innovation as a fundamental part of their journey. He envisioned a roadmap that would help them navigate the challenges and opportunities of the modern business landscape while continually adapting and evolving to solve tomorrow's problems.

The bustling coffee shop was now a backdrop to Mark's deep thoughts and ambitious vision. As he continued to outline the chapter, he couldn't help but feel a renewed sense of purpose and determination. The path to entrepreneurial success was paved with innovation, and he was eager to explore it, share his insights, and inspire others to do the same.

With a final sip of cappuccino, Mark saved his work and closed his laptop. Chapter 1 was well underway, and he knew it was just the beginning of an exciting journey to unravel the mysteries of innovation for entrepreneurs.

2

Navigating the Innovation Landscape

In the early light of a new day, Mark Harrison's excitement for his entrepreneurial journey continued to grow. He had just completed Chapter 1 of his book, "Solving Tomorrow's Problems: Innovation for Entrepreneurs," and was eager to dive deeper into the world of innovation. As he sat down at his desk, he contemplated what Chapter 2, "Navigating the Innovation Landscape," would entail.

The Innovation Ecosystem

Mark knew that to truly understand innovation, one must first comprehend the innovation ecosystem. This ecosystem was a complex web of interconnected entities, each playing a crucial role in the process of turning ideas into reality. From entrepreneurs and startups to research institutions, government agencies, investors, and customers, everyone had a part to play.

Entrepreneurs, as the driving force of innovation, needed to navigate this ecosystem skillfully. They had to identify the right partners, leverage available resources, and build relationships that would foster their ideas and businesses. Mark believed that an in-depth exploration of the innovation ecosystem would be invaluable to aspiring entrepreneurs.

The Role of Research and Development

One of the key elements of the innovation landscape was research and development (R&D). Mark was fascinated by how R&D could lead to groundbreaking discoveries and innovative solutions. Whether it was in a laboratory, a garage, or a co-working space, R&D was the engine that powered many successful innovations.

Mark knew that not all entrepreneurs had the resources to build extensive R&D departments, but he was convinced that there were creative ways to embrace the principles of research and development. Crowdsourcing, open innovation, and collaboration with academic institutions were just a few strategies that could help entrepreneurs tap into the power of R&D.

Embracing Risk and Uncertainty

As he researched for this chapter, Mark also delved into the concept of risk and uncertainty. He understood that the path of innovation was riddled with both. However, he believed that it was precisely in the face of these challenges that true innovation thrived. Entrepreneurs who embraced risk and uncertainty, rather than shying away from them, were often the ones who made the most significant breakthroughs.

Mark intended to explore various risk management strategies, from lean startup principles to scenario planning. He wanted to provide practical advice for entrepreneurs on how to take calculated risks, learn from their failures, and persevere when the road ahead seemed uncertain.

Funding and Investment

A critical aspect of navigating the innovation landscape was securing the necessary funding and investment. Mark knew that having a great idea was not enough; entrepreneurs needed financial support to bring their ideas to life. He aimed to shed light on the various funding options available, from bootstrapping and angel investors to venture capital and crowdfunding.

Mark also wanted to discuss the importance of demonstrating the potential for return on investment to potential funders. He would delve into crafting effective pitches and business plans, ensuring that entrepreneurs could communicate their vision and passion to potential investors.

Intellectual Property and Innovation

Protecting intellectual property (IP) was another vital topic on Mark's radar. He understood that entrepreneurs needed to safeguard their innovative ideas and creations from imitation or theft. He planned to cover the different forms of IP protection, such as patents, trademarks, copyrights, and trade secrets, and guide entrepreneurs on when and how to use them effectively.

Chapter 2 would also explore the ethical aspects of IP, encouraging entrepreneurs to respect the intellectual property rights of others while defending their own.

The Innovation Mindset

Ultimately, Mark believed that an innovation mindset was at the heart of successful entrepreneurship. In this chapter, he would highlight the qualities and habits that entrepreneurs needed to cultivate, such as curiosity, adaptability, resilience, and a commitment to lifelong learning. He was convinced that these qualities, when combined with the right knowledge and resources, could empower entrepreneurs to navigate the innovation landscape and overcome its challenges.

As Mark typed out the outline for Chapter 2, he couldn't help but feel a deep sense of purpose. Navigating the innovation landscape was a complex endeavor, but he was determined to provide aspiring entrepreneurs with the knowledge and tools they needed to succeed. This chapter would serve as a beacon, guiding them through the intricate terrain of innovation and helping them unlock their full entrepreneurial potential.

3

Ideation and Creativity: Seeds of Innovation

In the early hours of another day, Mark Harrison sat down to continue his exploration of the entrepreneurial journey in Chapter 3 of his book, "Solving Tomorrow's Problems: Innovation for Entrepreneurs." He knew that the seeds of innovation lay in the creative minds of entrepreneurs, and the chapter's title, "Ideation and Creativity: Seeds of Innovation," captured this essence.

The Power of Ideation

Mark recognized that every innovative venture began with an idea. Whether it was a revolutionary product, a new service, or a disruptive business model, it all started as a spark of creativity in someone's mind. Ideation was the process of generating, developing, and refining these ideas.

Mark believed that the ability to come up with fresh, unique, and impactful ideas was a critical skill for entrepreneurs. In this chapter, he would explore various techniques and strategies for ideation, from brainstorming sessions to mind mapping and beyond. He would also emphasize the importance of creating an environment that nurtured creativity and encouraged free thinking.

Problem-Solving as a Source of Innovation

One of the fundamental drivers of innovation was solving real-world problems. Mark was passionate about the idea that entrepreneurs had the power to identify existing challenges and develop innovative solutions to address them. In this chapter, he would discuss the art of problem-solving, emphasizing the need for empathy to truly understand the pain points of potential customers.

He would delve into the methods for conducting customer research, collecting feedback, and empathizing with the target audience. Mark believed that entrepreneurs who could pinpoint the most pressing problems were more likely to create solutions that resonated with the market.

The Role of Creativity

Creativity was the lifeblood of innovation, and Mark was eager to explore this concept in depth. He knew that many aspiring entrepreneurs might feel that creativity was a mysterious trait reserved for a select few. However, he believed that creativity was a skill that could be developed and honed.

The chapter would provide practical exercises and techniques to boost creative thinking. Mark wanted to encourage entrepreneurs to think beyond the obvious, embrace experimentation, and take inspiration from diverse sources. He would also highlight the importance of fostering a creative culture within a team or organization.

Nurturing an Idea to Innovation

An idea, no matter how brilliant, was only the beginning. The journey from idea to innovation required diligent nurturing. Mark planned to discuss the steps involved in refining and developing an idea, transforming it into a viable product or service.

This part of the chapter would cover aspects like conducting feasibility studies, prototyping, and iterating. Mark would emphasize the value of seeking early feedback, learning from mistakes, and continuously improving the idea. He knew that the path from idea to innovation was rarely straightforward, but with the right strategies, it could be a rewarding and transformative process.

Collaborative Innovation

Mark believed that innovation was not solely an individual endeavor. Collaboration and teamwork played a significant role in fostering new ideas and taking them to the next level. He would discuss the benefits of collaboration with co-founders, team members, mentors, and even competitors. Open-mindedness, effective communication, and a shared vision would be key components of this discussion.

Overcoming Creative Blocks

The creative process was not without its challenges. Mark intended to address common obstacles entrepreneurs might face, such as creative blocks and self-doubt. He would offer techniques for overcoming these hurdles and maintaining the creative momentum needed for innovative success.

As Mark continued to flesh out the chapter, he was energized by the thought of helping aspiring entrepreneurs unlock their creative potential. He knew that, by providing the tools and knowledge to foster ideation and creativity, he could empower them to turn their ideas into innovations that could shape the future. Chapter 3 was poised to be a guide to cultivate the seeds of innovation in the minds of ambitious entrepreneurs.

4

From Idea to Execution: Building Your Innovation

As the sun dipped below the horizon, Mark Harrison settled into his writing routine for Chapter 4 of his book, "Solving Tomorrow's Problems: Innovation for Entrepreneurs." The title of this chapter, "From Idea to Execution: Building Your Innovation," encapsulated the critical transition that every entrepreneur faced in their journey to bring their innovative ideas to life.

Defining Your Vision

Mark knew that the path from idea to execution was often fraught with uncertainty. To navigate this phase successfully, entrepreneurs needed a clear vision. In this chapter, he would delve into the process of defining and refining the vision for an innovative project. He would explore the importance of setting specific, measurable, achievable, relevant, and time-bound (SMART) goals, and how they could guide an entrepreneur's efforts.

Mark was passionate about the need for a well-defined mission and a clear sense of purpose. He believed that these factors were essential not only for staying motivated but also for effectively communicating the vision to potential collaborators, team members, and investors.

Building Your Team

Entrepreneurship was rarely a solitary journey. Collaborating with the right team members was crucial to executing an innovative idea successfully. In this chapter, Mark would discuss the process of assembling and leading a team, emphasizing the importance of diversity in skills, experience, and perspectives.

Mark would provide insights on recruitment, fostering a culture of innovation within the team, and effective leadership in the entrepreneurial context. He knew that the right team could make the difference between a good idea and a groundbreaking innovation.

Project Management and Planning

Turning an idea into an innovation required careful planning and effective project management. Mark would explore various project management methodologies and tools that could help entrepreneurs execute their vision efficiently. Concepts like agile and lean project management would be discussed, along with practical advice on how to adapt these approaches to the unique needs of innovative projects.

Mark recognized the value of a well-structured project plan, including budgeting, timelines, and milestones. He would highlight the importance of flexibility, as innovative projects often required adaptation to changing circumstances.

Prototyping and Minimum Viable Product (MVP)

The chapter would also delve into the concepts of prototyping and building a Minimum Viable Product (MVP). Mark understood that these strategies were instrumental in testing and refining innovative ideas. He would provide guidance on creating prototypes to visualize and test concepts and developing MVPs to collect valuable user feedback.

Mark believed that iterative development, which involved learning from user feedback and making continuous improvements, was essential for the success of innovative projects. He would share case studies and best practices to illustrate these concepts in action.

Scaling and Growth

Once an innovation had proven its value, it was time to scale and grow. Mark planned to discuss the strategies and challenges involved in scaling a business, expanding a customer base, and reaching new markets. This part of the chapter would also cover topics like funding for growth, partnerships, and international expansion.

Maintaining Innovation Momentum

Mark understood that maintaining the innovative spirit throughout the execution phase was critical. In this chapter, he would offer advice on fostering a culture of innovation within an organization and dealing with potential roadblocks and setbacks. He would provide insights into staying adaptable, responsive to changing market dynamics, and continuously improving.

As Mark crafted the content for Chapter 4, he couldn't help but feel the weight of the responsibility he had taken on. Empowering aspiring entrepreneurs to transition from idea to execution and build their innovations was a noble endeavor, and he was determined to provide them with the guidance and knowledge they needed to make this transformative leap. Chapter 4 was destined to be a roadmap for bringing dreams and ideas to life, creating innovations that would shape the future.

5

Market Entry and Innovation Adoption

As the sun cast long shadows in Mark Harrison's workspace, he began to work on Chapter 5 of his book, "Solving Tomorrow's Problems: Innovation for Entrepreneurs." The chapter, titled "Market Entry and Innovation Adoption," would explore the crucial steps and strategies involved in taking an innovative product or service to market and ensuring its widespread adoption.

Understanding Market Dynamics

Mark knew that successful innovation required a deep understanding of the target market. In this chapter, he would emphasize the importance of market research and analysis. He would guide aspiring entrepreneurs in identifying market trends, customer needs, and potential competition. Mark believed that this research was the foundation upon which a successful market entry strategy could be built.

Market Entry Strategies

Bringing innovation to market was not a one-size-fits-all endeavor. Mark intended to discuss various market entry strategies, ranging from disruptive market entry to incremental and niche strategies. He would explore the advantages and challenges associated with each approach and provide real-world examples to illustrate their effectiveness.

Mark believed that choosing the right market entry strategy was a critical decision for entrepreneurs, one that could significantly impact the success and sustainability of their innovation.

Building a Go-to-Market Plan

A well-crafted go-to-market (GTM) plan was essential for introducing an innovation to the market effectively. Mark planned to delve into the key elements of a GTM plan, such as pricing, distribution channels, marketing, and sales strategies. He would provide a step-by-step guide on how to develop a GTM plan tailored to the unique needs of an innovative product or service.

Overcoming Adoption Challenges

Mark knew that innovation adoption could face resistance and skepticism, especially if it represented a significant departure from the status quo. In this chapter, he would discuss common challenges to innovation adoption and provide strategies for overcoming them. He would explore concepts like the diffusion of innovation and discuss how to leverage early adopters and influencers to gain market traction.

Customer-Centric Innovation

Mark believed that successful market entry required a customer-centric approach. He would highlight the importance of understanding customer needs and preferences, designing a compelling user experience, and continually gathering feedback to improve the innovation. He would also emphasize the role of customer feedback in refining the innovation and making it more appealing to the target audience.

Sustaining Innovation

Innovation was not a one-time event; it required ongoing efforts to stay competitive and relevant. Mark would discuss the importance of sustaining innovation over time, encouraging entrepreneurs to keep their offerings fresh and responsive to changing market dynamics.

He would explore strategies for staying ahead of the competition, such as continuous improvement, expansion into new markets, and adapting to emerging trends. Mark was passionate about the idea that sustained innovation was not only about maintaining market share but also about creating a lasting impact.

Measuring Success

Finally, Mark planned to discuss methods for measuring the success of an innovation in the market. He would introduce key performance indicators (KPIs) and metrics that could help entrepreneurs gauge the effectiveness of their market entry and innovation adoption efforts. These metrics would cover aspects like customer acquisition, retention, revenue growth, and market share.

As Mark continued to work on Chapter 5, he was determined to provide aspiring entrepreneurs with the knowledge and strategies they needed to navigate the complex landscape of market entry and innovation adoption. He believed that this chapter would empower them to introduce their innovations to the world successfully, driving meaningful change and growth in the process.

6

Innovation and Sustainability: Making a Lasting Impact

As Mark Harrison embarked on writing Chapter 6 of his book, "Solving Tomorrow's Problems: Innovation for Entrepreneurs," he contemplated the critical role that sustainability played in the world of entrepreneurship. The title of this chapter, "Innovation and Sustainability: Making a Lasting Impact," underscored the profound impact that sustainable business practices could have on the future.

The Imperative of Sustainability

Mark believed that entrepreneurs had a responsibility to consider the environmental, social, and economic impact of their innovations. Sustainability was not just a buzzword but a fundamental aspect of building a business with a lasting legacy. In this chapter, he would explore the reasons why sustainability was essential, not only for the planet but also for the long-term success of a business.

Mark would discuss the United Nations' Sustainable Development Goals

(SDGs) and how entrepreneurs could align their innovations with these global objectives. He would also touch on the triple bottom line concept, which emphasized the importance of people, planet, and profit in business decision-making.

Sustainable Innovation Practices

Mark intended to provide practical guidance on how to integrate sustainability into the innovation process. He would explore sustainable design principles, eco-friendly materials, and energy-efficient technologies. He would also discuss circular economy models that focused on reducing waste and maximizing resource efficiency.

In addition, he would delve into the concept of "cradle-to-cradle" design, emphasizing the need for products and services to be designed with the end of their lifecycle in mind, ensuring that they could be recycled or repurposed.

Impactful Social Responsibility

Sustainability extended beyond environmental considerations. Mark believed that entrepreneurs should also address social issues through their innovations. He would discuss the concept of corporate social responsibility (CSR) and how businesses could contribute to the betterment of society.

The chapter would explore topics like ethical sourcing, fair labor practices, and community engagement. Mark would provide examples of companies that had successfully integrated social responsibility into their business models, and he would guide entrepreneurs on how to identify and support social causes aligned with their vision.

The Business Case for Sustainability

Mark was convinced that sustainability was not at odds with profitability.

In fact, he believed that sustainable business practices could enhance an organization's financial performance. He would discuss the business case for sustainability, including cost savings, market differentiation, and brand enhancement.

Mark would provide evidence from successful companies that had integrated sustainability into their operations and enjoyed both economic and environmental benefits. He would also share strategies for reducing waste, optimizing supply chains, and creating sustainable products and services.

Leveraging Technology for Sustainable Innovation

Technology played a pivotal role in driving sustainable innovation. Mark would explore how advances in technology, including artificial intelligence, the Internet of Things, and renewable energy solutions, could be harnessed to create innovative, sustainable solutions. He would also provide insights into the role of data analytics in sustainability efforts, helping entrepreneurs make data-driven decisions to reduce their environmental footprint.

Measuring and Reporting Sustainability

To ensure that sustainability efforts were meaningful, Mark would discuss the importance of measuring and reporting sustainability metrics. He would introduce key performance indicators (KPIs) for tracking environmental and social impact. He believed that transparent reporting was essential for accountability and for building trust with customers, investors, and other stakeholders.

Mark intended to conclude the chapter with inspiring case studies of businesses that had made a significant, positive impact through sustainable innovation. These stories would serve as a testament to the potential for entrepreneurs to create innovations that not only addressed today's challenges but also built a better future for generations to come.

Chapter 6 was poised to be a call to action, urging entrepreneurs to embrace sustainability as a cornerstone of their innovations and to use their businesses as a force for good in the world.

7

Innovation in a Changing World: Adapting to Challenges

As Mark Harrison continued his work on the book, "Solving Tomorrow's Problems: Innovation for Entrepreneurs," he knew that addressing the ever-evolving challenges in the entrepreneurial landscape was crucial. Chapter 7, titled "Innovation in a Changing World: Adapting to Challenges," would explore how entrepreneurs could navigate and thrive in a world filled with uncertainties and disruptions.

The Rapidly Changing Landscape

Mark understood that the world was in a constant state of flux. Technological advancements, economic shifts, and unforeseen events could significantly impact businesses. In this chapter, he would delve into the key challenges that entrepreneurs faced in a dynamic environment and provide strategies for adapting to these changes.

Embracing Disruption

Disruption, rather than being a barrier to success, could be an opportunity for innovation. Mark intended to discuss the concept of disruptive innovation and how entrepreneurs could use it to their advantage. He would provide examples of companies that had successfully disrupted traditional industries by identifying unmet needs and creating innovative solutions.

Resilience in the Face of Adversity

Entrepreneurship was not without its setbacks and challenges. Mark would explore the importance of resilience in overcoming adversity. He would discuss strategies for bouncing back from failures, learning from mistakes, and maintaining a positive mindset when faced with difficult circumstances.

Adapting to Technological Advancements

The rapid pace of technological advancement could be both an opportunity and a challenge for entrepreneurs. In this chapter, Mark would discuss the importance of staying up-to-date with emerging technologies and understanding how they could impact business operations and opportunities. He would also provide insights into leveraging technology for competitive advantage.

Navigating Economic Shifts

Economic fluctuations were a common occurrence in the business world. Mark would explore strategies for managing financial risks, adapting business models, and identifying new revenue streams during economic downturns. He would emphasize the importance of financial planning, including building robust cash reserves and diversifying revenue sources.

The Role of Regulation and Compliance

Regulations and compliance requirements varied across industries and regions, posing unique challenges to entrepreneurs. Mark would provide guidance on staying informed about relevant regulations, maintaining compliance, and understanding the potential impact of legislative changes on business operations. He would also explore the benefits of ethical and transparent business practices.

Building a Culture of Innovation

To thrive in a changing world, Mark believed that businesses needed to foster a culture of innovation within their organizations. He would discuss how to encourage creative thinking, adaptability, and a willingness to experiment among team members. Mark would provide strategies for building innovative cultures that were resilient in the face of change.

Preparing for the Unpredictable

The chapter would also address the importance of contingency planning and risk management. Mark would discuss how to prepare for unforeseen events, from natural disasters to global pandemics. He would emphasize the value of having robust contingency plans in place to ensure business continuity.

Collaborative Adaptation

Mark was aware that entrepreneurs could not face the challenges of a changing world in isolation. Collaboration and partnerships were crucial to adapting to new circumstances. He would explore the benefits of forming strategic alliances, sharing resources, and tapping into collective knowledge to address challenges.

Chapter 7 would be a guide to helping entrepreneurs build the resilience and adaptability needed to thrive in an ever-changing business landscape. It would underscore the idea that in the face of uncertainty, innovation was not a luxury but a necessity for long-term success.

8

Innovation for the Future: Trends and Emerging Opportunities

As Mark Harrison penned the opening lines of Chapter 8, titled "Innovation for the Future: Trends and Emerging Opportunities," he couldn't help but feel a sense of excitement about the possibilities that lay ahead. This chapter would delve into the forward-looking aspects of innovation, exploring emerging trends and the opportunities they presented for entrepreneurs.

The Acceleration of Change

Mark began by acknowledging the accelerated pace of change in today's world. Technological advancements, cultural shifts, and global events were shaping the future faster than ever before. He would discuss the implications of this acceleration for entrepreneurs and how staying attuned to change was a critical skill for innovation.

Emerging Technology Trends

The chapter would dive into the most impactful emerging technologies and trends, including artificial intelligence, blockchain, quantum computing, biotechnology, and more. Mark would explore how these technologies could revolutionize industries and create new opportunities for entrepreneurs. He would provide practical insights into how entrepreneurs could leverage these trends to drive innovation in their businesses.

Sustainability and Environmental Innovation

Sustainability remained a central theme as Mark delved into the future of innovation. He would discuss how the growing focus on sustainability and environmental concerns was driving innovation in industries such as renewable energy, circular economy practices, and eco-friendly product development. He would also explore how entrepreneurs could contribute to a more sustainable future.

Healthcare and Biomedical Innovation

The healthcare and biomedical sectors were experiencing rapid transformation. Mark would examine the potential for innovative breakthroughs in personalized medicine, telehealth, and genomics. He would provide insights into how entrepreneurs could tap into the evolving healthcare landscape and contribute to improved patient outcomes and healthcare delivery.

The Rise of Artificial Intelligence

Artificial intelligence (AI) was a force with the potential to reshape countless industries. Mark would explore AI's impact on areas like automation, data analytics, and predictive modeling. He would provide guidance on how entrepreneurs could integrate AI into their businesses, improve decision-making, and enhance customer experiences.

E-Commerce and Online Marketplaces

E-commerce and online marketplaces were experiencing significant growth. Mark would discuss the opportunities for entrepreneurs in these spaces, including niche markets, dropshipping, and direct-to-consumer business models. He would provide strategies for entrepreneurs looking to establish and grow their online presence.

The Future of Work and Remote Collaboration

Remote work and digital collaboration were transforming the way businesses operated. Mark would delve into the future of work, exploring trends like remote teams, digital nomadism, and the gig economy. He would discuss how entrepreneurs could adapt to these changes and leverage remote collaboration for innovation.

Space Exploration and Extraterrestrial Innovation

The final frontier was opening up new possibilities for innovation. Mark would discuss the burgeoning space industry and how it offered opportunities in fields such as space tourism, asteroid mining, and satellite technology. He would encourage entrepreneurs to consider the possibilities of innovation beyond Earth.

Ethical Considerations in Future Innovation

Innovation for the future also came with ethical considerations. Mark would address topics like data privacy, AI ethics, and responsible technology development. He would emphasize the importance of considering ethical implications in innovation and promoting responsible business practices.

Chapter 8 was designed to inspire entrepreneurs to look beyond the present and explore the exciting possibilities that the future held. Mark's aim was to equip them with the knowledge and insights needed to seize emerging opportunities, adapt to evolving trends, and drive innovation that would shape the world of tomorrow.

9

Innovation for Impact: Making a Difference in the World

As Mark Harrison approached Chapter 9 of his book, "Solving Tomorrow's Problems: Innovation for Entrepreneurs," he knew it was time to explore the profound impact that innovation could have on the world. The title, "Innovation for Impact: Making a Difference in the World," underscored the transformational role that entrepreneurs could play in solving pressing global challenges.

The Power of Purpose-Driven Innovation

Mark believed that innovation driven by a higher purpose could be a powerful force for good. In this chapter, he would discuss how entrepreneurs could infuse their innovations with a sense of purpose, aligning their businesses with causes that mattered to them. He would provide examples of purpose-driven companies that had made a meaningful impact.

Innovations for Social Good

Mark was passionate about the potential for entrepreneurs to address social and humanitarian challenges through innovation. He would explore areas like education, healthcare, clean energy, and poverty alleviation, discussing how innovative solutions could drive positive change. Mark would provide insights into funding sources and organizations that supported social impact innovation.

Philanthropy and Corporate Social Responsibility

Entrepreneurs who achieved success often had the opportunity to give back. Mark would discuss the role of philanthropy and corporate social responsibility in making a difference. He would provide guidance on how entrepreneurs could establish charitable foundations, support meaningful causes, and use their resources to impact society positively.

Environmental Stewardship

Sustainability and environmental responsibility were central to this chapter. Mark would delve into how entrepreneurs could contribute to environmental stewardship through eco-friendly products, green practices, and conservation efforts. He would also discuss the importance of investing in renewable energy and reducing carbon footprints.

Global Challenges and Entrepreneurial Solutions

The world faced an array of global challenges, from climate change to healthcare disparities and access to clean water. Mark intended to explore how entrepreneurs could address these challenges through innovative solutions. He would discuss the United Nations' Sustainable Development Goals and how entrepreneurs could contribute to these global initiatives.

The Role of Technology in Humanitarian Aid

Technology could be a game-changer in humanitarian aid efforts. Mark would examine the use of technology in disaster relief, refugee support, and healthcare access in underserved regions. He would provide examples of entrepreneurs and organizations that were making a difference in the humanitarian sector through innovative tech solutions.

Innovation and Education

Education was a fundamental driver of positive change. Mark would explore how entrepreneurs could innovate in the education sector, whether through e-learning platforms, educational content, or vocational training. He would discuss the importance of improving access to quality education for all.

Creating a Legacy of Impact

In the final section of the chapter, Mark would discuss how entrepreneurs could leave a lasting legacy of impact. He would explore the concept of social entrepreneurship and how businesses could be vehicles for positive change. Mark would encourage entrepreneurs to consider the long-term societal impact of their innovations.

Chapter 9 was designed to inspire and guide entrepreneurs to use their innovative power to make a difference in the world. It would serve as a call to action, challenging entrepreneurs to think beyond profits and recognize the potential of their innovations to address the most significant challenges facing humanity.

10

The Entrepreneur's Toolkit: Strategies for Success

In this chapter, we'll delve into the practical strategies, skills, and tools that every entrepreneur should have in their toolkit. These are the essential elements that can make the difference between success and failure in the dynamic and competitive world of entrepreneurship.

Building a Strong Business Plan

A solid business plan is the foundation of any successful venture. In this section, we'll explore the key components of a business plan, from defining your business concept to outlining your market strategy and financial projections. We'll provide practical tips on how to create a business plan that not only guides your business but also attracts investors and partners.

Marketing and Branding Strategies

Effective marketing and branding are critical for getting your product or service noticed and establishing a strong presence in the market. We'll discuss strategies for identifying your target audience, creating a compelling brand identity, and developing marketing campaigns that resonate with your customers. We'll also explore digital marketing, social media, and content marketing as essential tools for modern entrepreneurs.

Financial Management and Budgeting

Financial management is at the heart of a successful business. In this section, we'll delve into topics such as budgeting, financial forecasting, and cash flow management. We'll provide insights on how to keep your business financially healthy and sustainable, even in challenging times. We'll also discuss the importance of seeking funding and the different options available to entrepreneurs.

Sales and Customer Relationship Management

Sales are the lifeblood of any business, and effective sales strategies are crucial for growth. We'll explore the art of sales, from prospecting and lead generation to closing deals and building long-term customer relationships. We'll also discuss the role of customer relationship management (CRM) software in streamlining your sales processes.

Networking and Relationship Building

Building a strong network is essential for entrepreneurs. We'll provide tips on how to expand your professional network, whether through local events, industry conferences, or online platforms. We'll discuss the power of building strategic relationships with mentors, advisors, and fellow entrepreneurs.

Time Management and Productivity

Time is a precious resource for entrepreneurs, and effective time management is key to achieving your goals. We'll explore time management techniques, including prioritization, goal setting, and productivity tools. We'll provide strategies for balancing your personal and professional life and avoiding burnout.

Problem-Solving and Adaptability

Entrepreneurship often involves navigating obstacles and challenges. We'll discuss problem-solving techniques and how to adapt to changing circumstances. We'll emphasize the importance of resilience and a growth mindset in overcoming setbacks and embracing change.

Negotiation and Communication Skills

Effective negotiation and communication are critical in various aspects of entrepreneurship, from securing deals with suppliers and partners to leading your team and addressing customer concerns. We'll provide insights on negotiation strategies and how to communicate persuasively and diplomatically.

Legal and Intellectual Property Considerations

Understanding legal and intellectual property (IP) matters is crucial for protecting your business and innovations. We'll discuss the basics of business law, contracts, and the importance of safeguarding your intellectual property through patents, trademarks, and copyrights.

Leadership and Team Building

Entrepreneurs often find themselves in leadership roles, whether they're leading a team of employees or collaborators. We'll explore the principles of effective leadership, team building, and creating a positive workplace culture.

Leveraging Technology

In the digital age, technology can be a powerful ally for entrepreneurs. We'll discuss how to leverage technology for efficiency, automation, and data-driven decision-making. We'll explore the use of software and tools for various aspects of your business, from project management to customer support.

Chapter 10 aims to equip entrepreneurs with the practical knowledge and skills they need to succeed in their entrepreneurial journey. It's a comprehensive toolkit that covers the essential elements of building and growing a successful business.

11

Beyond Entrepreneurship: Scaling and Legacy

In this final chapter of "Solving Tomorrow's Problems: Innovation for Entrepreneurs," we will explore the transition from being an entrepreneur to becoming a business leader and the legacy you can create. This chapter delves into how you can scale your impact, ensure long-term success, and leave a lasting mark on the world.

Scaling Your Business

Scaling your business is about taking it to the next level. We'll discuss strategies for growth, including expanding into new markets, diversifying your product or service offerings, and acquiring or merging with other businesses. Scaling also involves fine-tuning your operations, optimizing efficiency, and ensuring your team is ready for growth.

Leadership at Scale

As your business grows, your role as a leader evolves. We'll explore the challenges of leading a larger organization, including managing teams, fostering a culture of innovation, and inspiring employees. We'll discuss how to maintain a strong vision and adapt to the changing needs of your company.

Exit Strategies and Succession Planning

At some point, you may consider exiting your business, whether through a sale, merger, or passing it on to the next generation. We'll provide insights into exit strategies and the importance of succession planning to ensure a smooth transition and protect your legacy.

Social and Environmental Responsibility

We'll revisit the concept of corporate social responsibility and environmental sustainability, emphasizing how established businesses can continue to make a positive impact. We'll discuss how to integrate social and environmental responsibility into your business operations and create a legacy of ethical and sustainable practices.

Mentorship and Giving Back

As an accomplished entrepreneur, you have the opportunity to mentor the next generation of innovators and give back to your community. We'll explore the benefits of mentorship and ways to support emerging entrepreneurs through your experience and resources.

Personal and Professional Growth

Your journey as an entrepreneur is a continuous learning experience. We'll discuss the importance of personal and professional growth, from furthering your education to expanding your horizons. We'll explore how ongoing development can empower you to tackle new challenges and adapt to a changing business landscape.

Leaving a Lasting Legacy

Leaving a lasting legacy is the culmination of your entrepreneurial journey. We'll reflect on the impact you've made, the innovation you've driven, and the positive change you've created. We'll discuss the various ways you can cement your legacy, from philanthropy to initiatives that reflect your values and passions.

Staying Connected

Entrepreneurship can be an isolating endeavor. We'll emphasize the value of staying connected with the entrepreneurial community and finding ways to share your knowledge, experience, and insights with others.

Reflecting on Your Journey

We'll conclude the chapter and the book by encouraging you to reflect on your entrepreneurial journey. We'll ask you to consider the challenges you've overcome, the lessons you've learned, and the impact you've had. We'll prompt you to think about your vision for the future and how you want to be remembered as an entrepreneur.

Chapter 11 serves as a guide to help you transition from the initial stages of entrepreneurship to becoming a seasoned leader and a force for positive change. It's a reminder that your entrepreneurial journey is not just about building a business but also about leaving a lasting legacy that shapes the world for the better.

12

Summary

"Solving Tomorrow's Problems: Innovation for Entrepreneurs" is a comprehensive guide that takes aspiring entrepreneurs and business leaders on a journey through the world of innovation and entrepreneurship. Each chapter of the book is designed to equip readers with the knowledge and strategies they need to succeed in the dynamic and competitive realm of entrepreneurship.

Here's a summary of the key themes and concepts explored in each chapter:

1. Chapter 1: Solving Tomorrow's Problems: Innovation for Entrepreneurs
   - Introduction to the book's focus on innovation and entrepreneurship.
   - The importance of innovation in addressing future challenges.

2. Chapter 2: The Entrepreneurial Mindset: Cultivating the Seeds of Innovation
   - Exploring the entrepreneurial mindset and the qualities that drive innovation.
   - Strategies for fostering creativity, adaptability, and resilience.

3. Chapter 3: Ideation and Creativity: Seeds of Innovation
   - The process of generating, developing, and refining innovative ideas.

SUMMARY

   - Problem-solving as a source of innovation and techniques for creative thinking.

4. Chapter 4: From Idea to Execution: Building Your Innovation
   - Transitioning from idea to execution, including defining a vision and building a team.
   - Project management, prototyping, and scaling strategies for bringing innovations to life.

5. Chapter 5: Market Entry and Innovation Adoption
   - Understanding market dynamics and entry strategies.
   - Strategies for successfully adopting and marketing innovations in a competitive landscape.

6. Chapter 6: Innovation and Sustainability: Making a Lasting Impact
   - The importance of sustainability and its impact on the future of business.
   - Strategies for integrating sustainability and social responsibility into innovation.

7. Chapter 7: Innovation in a Changing World: Adapting to Challenges
   - Navigating and thriving in a rapidly changing business landscape.
   - Strategies for embracing disruption and building resilience.

8. Chapter 8: Innovation for the Future: Trends and Emerging Opportunities
   - Exploring emerging technology trends and their potential impact on entrepreneurship.
   - Opportunities in sustainability, healthcare, AI, and more.

9. Chapter 9: Innovation for Impact: Making a Difference in the World
   - The power of purpose-driven innovation and creating innovations for social good.
   - Philanthropy, environmental stewardship, and contributing to global challenges.

10. Chapter 10: The Entrepreneur's Toolkit: Strategies for Success
   - Practical strategies and skills, including building a strong business plan, marketing, financial management, and time management.
   - Legal considerations, leadership, and leveraging technology.

11. Chapter 11: Beyond Entrepreneurship: Scaling and Legacy
   - Strategies for scaling a business, leadership at scale, and exit planning.
   - Social and environmental responsibility, mentorship, and personal growth.

12. Chapter 12: Conclusion - Reflecting on Your Journey
   - Wrapping up the entrepreneurial journey and leaving a lasting legacy.
   - The importance of reflection and staying connected with the entrepreneurial community.

Throughout the book, Mark Harrison provides practical advice, real-world examples, and actionable strategies to empower entrepreneurs to drive innovation, navigate challenges, and create a positive impact on the world. It serves as a comprehensive guide for both aspiring and seasoned entrepreneurs on their quest to solve tomorrow's problems through innovation.

www.ingramcontent.com/pod-product-compliance
Lightning Source LLC
LaVergne TN
LVHW010438070526
838199LV00066B/6071